Thomas Jefferson

Community BUILDERS

Thomas Jefferson

Community BUILDERS

Voice of Liberty

by
Andrew Santella

Children's Press®
A Division of Grolier Publishing
New York / London / Hong Kong / Sydney
Danbury, Connecticut

Photo Credits

Photographs ©: Archive Photos: back cover (Lambert), 33; Art Resource, NY: 27 right (National Museum of American Art, Washington DC), cover (National Portrait Gallery, Smithsonian Institution), 31; Christie's Images: 27 left (Artist: School of Joseph-Siffrede Duplessis); Corbis-Bettmann: 25 (Painting by Edgar Pine); Library of Congress: 20, 39; Mae Scanlan: 30; Monticello/Thomas Jefferson Memorial Foundation, Inc: 41 (Robert Lautman), 2 (Painting by Thomas Sully), 17; North Wind Picture Archives: 9, 16, 18, 23, 24, 28, 34, 35, 43; Stock Boston: 45 (Billy E. Barns), 44 (Bob Daemrich); Stock Montage, Inc.: 7, 15, 37, Superstock, Inc.: 10, 40; University of Virginia Library, Special Collections: 3; Virginia Tourism Corporation: 12, 14.

Reading Consultant

Linda Cornwell, Coordinator of School Quality and Professional Improvement, Indiana State Teachers Association

Visit Children's Press on the Internet at:
http://publishing.grolier.com

Library of Congress Cataloging-in-Publication Data

Santella, Andrew.
    Thomas Jefferson : voice of liberty / by Andrew Santella.
        p. cm. — (Community builders)
    Includes bibliographical references and index.
    Summary: A biography of the third president of the United States, covering his early life in Virginia, his authorship of the Declaration of Independence, his political career, his retirement to Monticello, and his founding of the University of Virginia.
    ISBN: 0-516-21587-6 (lib. bdg.) 0-516-26514-8 (pbk.)
    1. Jefferson, Thomas, 1743–1826—Juvenile literature. 2. Presidents—United States—Biography—Juvenile literature. [1. Jefferson, Thomas, 1743–1826. 2. Presidents.] I. Title. II. Series.
E332.79.S256 1999
973.4'6'092—dc21
[b]
                                                                            98-45700
                                                                                 CIP
                                                                                  AC

Contents

Chapter ONE

America's Guiding Vision

Thomas Jefferson spent the hot summer of 1776 in Philadelphia. He was there as one of Virginia's representatives in the Second Continental Congress. Leaders from each of Britain's thirteen American colonies were meeting to decide their political future. Jefferson knew the Congress would need his skills as a writer. He brought his own chair and writing desk to the rooms he rented in a three-story brick house at Market and Seventh

Delegates to the Second Continental Congress assembled in
1775 to discuss the future of the thirteen British colonies.

streets. In June, Jefferson sat at the desk and wrote
some of the most important words in American
history. He wrote the Declaration of Independence.

The Continental Congress

The Continental Congress was an assembly of representatives of Britain's American colonies. The First Continental Congress opened in Philadelphia on September 5, 1774. About fifty representatives came from twelve colonies. Their purpose was to decide what to do about the harsh measures Britain had imposed on the colonies to punish them for the Boston Tea Party. A second Congress began meeting on May 10, 1775. By this time, battles between the colonists and the British had already been fought at Lexington and Concord in Massachusetts. For the next six years, the Continental Congress directed the Revolutionary War and worked to preserve the union of thirteen colonies.

Thomas Jefferson's talents as a writer made him a valuable member of the Second Continental Congress.

Jefferson's words announced to the world that the American colonies were to be united as one independent nation. They declared that this new nation would be based on the equality of individuals and that it would protect their human rights.

The Declaration of Independence is among the most treasured documents in U.S. history.

Jefferson wrote: "We hold these truths to be self-evident, that all men are created equal, that they are endowed by their Creator with certain inalienable Rights, that among these are life, liberty and the pursuit of happiness. That to secure these rights, governments are instituted among men, deriving their just powers from the consent of the governed. . . ."

For more than 225 years, the United States has strived to live up to those words. The Declaration of Independence continues to be the guiding vision of American democracy.

10

Chapter TWO

Birth of a Revolution

Thomas Jefferson was born in Shadwell, in Goochland County, Virginia, on April 2, 1743. His father Peter was a wealthy planter and commander of the local militia (a military force that is ready for service in emergencies). His mother Jane was from one of the most well-known families in Virginia, the Randolphs. Thomas Jefferson grew up in wealth and privilege. Like most wealthy people in Virginia at that time, the Jeffersons owned many slaves. Later, Jefferson would inherit about twenty slaves from his father and about 135 slaves from his

Some of Virginia's farmland appears almost unchanged since the time when Jefferson's family inhabited it.

father-in-law. The man who would later write that "all men are created equal" owned slaves all his life.

As a young student, Jefferson was very serious about his education. He lived with a series of local schoolteachers. From them, he learned to read Latin, Greek, and French. When he was seventeen,

12

Jefferson's Slaves

Thomas Jefferson called slavery an "abominable crime." But he never freed his own slaves. At Jefferson's home, about eighty black slaves cared for his children and tended his crops. They even helped build his house, Monticello. About half of Jefferson's teenage male slaves were under the age of sixteen. They worked in a nail factory that Jefferson set up on his plantation.

he enrolled at the College of William and Mary in Williamsburg. Over the next two years, he studied science, math, and rhetoric (the use of language). In college, Jefferson spent many hours each day with his books. This left him time to do little else besides eat, sleep, and practice his violin. Even after he graduated, Jefferson wasn't finished with his studies. He spent five more years in Williamsburg studying law. It was as a law student that Jefferson watched Patrick Henry denounce the British Stamp Act in 1765 as unfair to the American colonists.

The College of William and Mary, founded in 1693, is one of the oldest educational institutions in the country.

The Stamp Act

The Stamp Act was passed by the British Parliament in 1765 as a way of taxing American colonists. Under the Stamp Act, colonists had to pay a fee on all legal documents, licenses, newspapers, and playing cards. Colonists argued that the tax wasn't fair because they weren't represented in Parliament.

Patrick Henry was a member of the Virginia House of Burgesses when he delivered his famous speech against the Stamp Act in 1765.

King George III
ruled England
from 1760
to 1820.

When Jefferson finally began his own law practice, he was quickly swept into politics. In 1769, he took his seat in the House of Burgesses, the legislative assembly of the colony of Virginia. He entered politics just as the conflict between American colonists and Great Britain's Parliament and King George III was heating up. Like many colonists, Jefferson believed Britain was

16

taking unfair advantage of its American colonies. He sought to protect the rights of the colonists. He opposed all forms of taxes imposed by the British Parliament against them. He supported action against British trade regulations.

Jefferson drew this sketch for the first version of Monticello sometime around 1769.

Monticello

Monticello gets its name from the Italian word for "little mountain." The main house is a three-story building with twenty-one rooms (plus twelve in the cellar) and topped by a dome. Jefferson began building the house in 1769. When his father's house burned down in 1771, Jefferson moved into the South Pavilion, the first finished building at Monticello. Jefferson worked on the house for most of his adult life. Work on the main house wasn't completed until 1809.

Today, Monticello is open to visitors throughout the year.

Around the same time, he decided to build a new home for himself. It would be on top of an 867-foot (264-meter)-high mountain on land he had inherited from his father. He would call it Monticello. Jefferson spent most of his life building and rebuilding the house. It became one of the most remarkable private homes in the young United States. Jefferson filled it with many interesting inventions—alcove beds (beds that were built into the wall), a dumb-waiter (a kind of small hand-pulled elevator that carried wine from the cellar to the dining room), and even a polygraph (a device that copied letters he wrote). At Monticello, Jefferson pursued his many interests, from architecture to botany (the study of plants) to book collecting. He rode horses through the countryside around the house and entertained guests at night. Monticello would always be his refuge from the turbulent world of politics.

On New Year's Day, 1772, Jefferson married Martha Wayles Skelton, a twenty-three-year-old widow. Their marriage was a happy one. At Monticello, the two liked to play music together—

Although there are no portraits of Jefferson's wife or children, this illustration of his daughter, Martha, was drawn about 1800.

Martha on the harpsichord (a keyboard instrument popular at the time) and Jefferson on the violin. Martha gave birth to six children, but only two survived to become adults. Martha "Patsy" Jefferson was born in 1772. Mary, called "Polly," was born in 1778.

Jefferson's wife Martha developed a number of health problems. She was sickly and weak through much of the marriage. When she died in 1782, Jefferson was crushed. He never remarried.

Jefferson's Library

Jefferson once wrote: "I cannot live without books." He called books "his chosen companions." He owned almost seven thousand of them and could read seven languages. He read every night before falling asleep. In 1815, he sold nearly all of his books to the United States government. They formed the main part of the Library of Congress collection. Some are still stored at the library in Washington, D.C., but most were destroyed in a fire in 1851.

Meanwhile, Jefferson was playing a bigger role in the movement toward American independence. In 1774, he wrote a series of instructions to Virginia representatives to the Continental Congress. Newspapers throughout the colonies printed the instructions called, *A Summary View of the Rights of British America.* Its message was simple: "The British parliament has no right to exercise authority over us." Jefferson argued that Parliament was trying to destroy colonial freedom. His writing put him at the forefront of the revolutionary movement.

In 1775, Jefferson was selected to represent Virginia in the Second Continental Congress in Philadelphia. He was a member of a group of representatives that included such famous men as Patrick Henry, Richard Henry Lee, and George Washington. By that time, the American colonies had not yet declared their independence, but the Revolutionary War had already begun. Battles had been fought in Massachusetts at Lexington, Concord, and Bunker Hill. George Washington had

The Revolutionary War began on April 19, 1775, when British soldiers and colonial militiamen clashed in the towns of Lexington and Concord, Massachusetts. Here, they fight at Concord Bridge.

gone to lead the Continental army outside Boston. One of the tasks facing the Second Continental Congress was to explain to the world why American colonists had taken up arms against the British. The leadership in Congress turned to Jefferson to set down on paper their reasons for fighting. His success with *A Summary View* made him a natural choice.

Jefferson produced a document called the *Declaration of the Causes and Necessity for Taking Up Arms*. It listed the colonists' complaints about their treatment at the hands of the British. It declared that their war was just and that the colonists could win it. Congress approved the document and adopted it as its official position on the war.

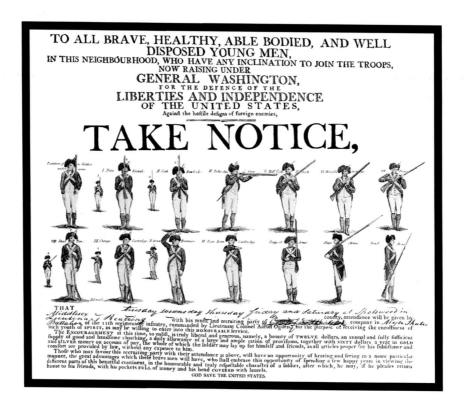

This recruiting poster, which shows colonial soldiers going through drills, calls on all brave, healthy, and able-bodied young men to join the troops and fight the British.

Members of the Second Continental Congress debate the issue of independence.

Jefferson rarely spoke during the debates on independence in Congress, but his talent as a writer made him an important delegate. Whenever a significant document needed to be written, Congress turned to Jefferson. This set the stage for his greatest achievement—the Declaration of Independence.

Chapter THREE

Author of the Declaration of Independence

By June 1776, the colonies were ready to completely break away from Great Britain. The Revolutionary War was in its second year. All that remained was for the Continental Congress to officially declare independence. Jefferson was appointed to a five-person committee that was asked to write the declaration. The committee members turned to Jefferson to do most of the writing. He was the perfect choice for the job. He completed a first draft on June 28. Then he showed it to Benjamin Franklin and John Adams,

Although Benjamin Franklin (left) and John Adams (right) suggested changes to Jefferson's declaration, Adams later called it "a masterful expression of the American mind."

who were also members of the committee. They suggested a few minor changes. The declaration was passed along to the entire Congress. After more changes were made, Congress approved it on July 4.

Philadelphians cheer after a reading of the newly adopted Declaration of Independence.

The Declaration of Independence assured Jefferson a place among America's great thinkers and leaders. In the summer of 1776, the declaration was read throughout the newly formed United States of America. The crowds of people rejoiced.

With his work done, Jefferson returned to Monticello at the end of the summer. He couldn't wait to see his family. But he also set about shaping the new state government in Virginia. He was a member of the Virginia General Assembly (the state's lawmaking body) from 1776 to 1779. He pro-

The Declaration of Independence

Jefferson kept a copy of the Declaration of Independence at Monticello to show visitors. The original document is displayed at the National Archives in Washington, D.C.

posed many changes to the state's laws. He wanted to give more owners of small farms the right to vote. He argued for complete religious freedom. He suggested overhauling criminal laws to limit the use of the death penalty. He urged Virginia to create a statewide public-school system. All of Jefferson's ideas had one thing in common: They encouraged individual freedom and achievement. He wanted to put into practice the ideas he set forth in the Declaration of Independence. Jefferson considered the bill establishing religious freedom in Virginia to be one of his greatest accomplishments. It stated that no one should suffer for his religious beliefs. The General Assembly, however, rejected many of Jefferson's plans. It would be years before a lot of them became law.

As governor, Jefferson spent much of his time at the Governor's Palace in Williamsburg, Virginia.

Jefferson also served as governor of Virginia from 1779 to 1781. It was a difficult time. The Revolutionary War was still raging. Many of Virginia's soldiers were fighting elsewhere. When the British army invaded Virginia in 1781, Jefferson himself narrowly escaped capture.

After the war ended in 1783, Jefferson served in the U.S. Congress. In 1784, he was sent to France as the United States's minister, or representative. He returned to the United States in 1789. While he was away, the United States had ratified, or approved, a Constitution. The Constitution gave the United States a new national government. Among other major changes, it created the office of president.

President George Washington (left) and his cabinet, including Thomas Jefferson (second from right), the first secretary of state

Secretary of State

The secretary of state is the president's chief adviser on foreign affairs and the highest ranking member of the cabinet. The secretary is appointed by the president, with the approval of the Senate.

When George Washington, the country's first president, had to select his cabinet (the government officers who would advise him in key areas), he chose Jefferson to be the first secretary of state. Jefferson worked in Washington's cabinet for three years.

In 1797, Jefferson ran for president of the United States and finished second to John Adams. At that time, the runner-up in the race for president became vice president. Jefferson served as vice president from 1797 to 1801.

Chapter FOUR

The Third President

Thomas Jefferson became the third president of the United States on March 4, 1801. He was the first president to serve his entire term in Washington, D.C., the country's new capital. Jefferson believed that as president he should not be a part of fancy ceremonies. At his inauguration, he decided not to have a formal parade. Instead he walked with friends from his boarding-

This portrait of Thomas Jefferson was painted during his presidency, which began in 1801.

**Washington, D.C., in 1800, around the time
it became the nation's capital**

house to the Capitol. Once he took office, he instructed that visitors should not bow to him, but shake his hand. He dressed simply instead of wearing expensive clothes. Everything he did was meant to suggest that he was a man of the people—not a kinglike authority.

Jefferson wasn't president long before his leadership was tested. Pirates from the African nation of

Tripoli demanded cash payments in return for not attacking U.S. ships. Jefferson sent a naval force to Tripoli to defeat the pirates. In 1805, the United States signed a peace treaty with Tripoli.

In 1803, Jefferson arranged to buy the Louisiana Territory from France for $15 million. The Louisiana Purchase nearly doubled the size of the United States. The purchase included territory

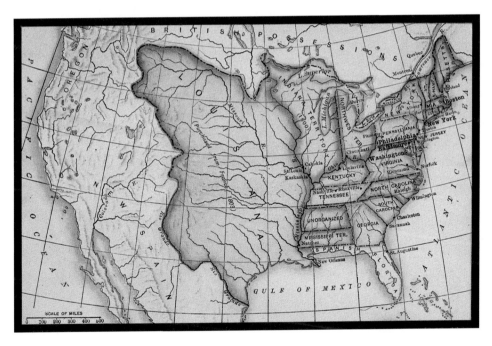

Acquiring the territory of Louisiana expanded the territory of the young United States from the Mississippi River to the Rocky Mountains.

much larger than the present-day state of Louisiana. The new land stretched from the Mississippi River to the Rocky Mountains. To explore it, Jefferson sent Meriwether Lewis, William Clark, and their crew on a journey to the Pacific Ocean and back.

The Lewis and Clark Expedition

The Lewis and Clark expedition was the first overland exploration of the American West by United States citizens. Beginning in May 1804, Lewis, Clark, and a group of about fifty people traveled from St. Louis, Missouri, along the Missouri River, over the Rocky Mountains, and all the way to the Pacific Ocean near present-day Astoria, Oregon. They returned to St. Louis in September 1806. The expedition spurred the United States's westward growth.

British naval officers seize an American sailor in order to force him to serve in the British navy.

Jefferson's second term as president (1805–09) was filled with trouble. The greatest crisis involved relations with Great Britain. The British stopped American ships at sea and forced many U.S. seamen to serve in their navy. Britain also interfered with American sea trade. To strike back, Jefferson urged Congress to pass the Embargo Act of 1807. The act stopped U.S. ships from sailing to foreign ports and closed U.S. ports to foreign vessels. The act was a disaster. The U.S. economy was shattered. Prices for crops fell. Merchants, shipbuilders, and farmers suffered. Many people lost their jobs. When Jefferson left the presidency in 1809, the Embargo Act expired.

Chapter FIVE

Retirement at Monticello

Jefferson left office in 1809. He retired to Monticello, but remained active. He turned to gardening, farming, and experimenting with new kinds of plants on his farm. He wrote thousands of letters and entertained many visitors.

In 1814, Jefferson began working on his "holy cause"—education. He urged Virginia to enact his plan for statewide public education. The legislature rejected much of Jefferson's plan, but it gave approval for a state university. Jefferson hired faculty from all over the world. He wrote the college's rules and regulations. He drew up the course of

When his presidency ended, Jefferson gladly returned to the work of life at Monticello, including farming, experimenting, and overseeing the work of his slaves.

Gardener and Farmer

Thomas Jefferson was an avid gardener and farmer. He was interested in finding ways to improve tools used for farming. In 1788, he began working on a new kind of moldboard for plows. (The moldboard is the part of the plow that turns soil over once it has been cut.) He began using his own invention in 1794. It received a gold medal from The French Society of Agriculture.

The University of Virginia

Thomas Jefferson called opening the University of Virginia "the last act of usefulness I can render." He said that if he could see it open, "he would not ask an hour more of life." Today, more than eighteen thousand students are enrolled at the university.

The University of Virginia library, one of the buildings Jefferson designed

study. He designed the campus buildings. In 1819, the University of Virginia was founded. Through a telescope, Jefferson could see the school from his home a few miles away.

Jefferson's last years were spent in poor health. By July 1826, he was on his deathbed. The fiftieth anniversary of the Declaration of Independence was approaching. As he became sicker, Jefferson began slipping in and out of sleep. Late on July 3rd, he woke and asked his doctors, "Is it the fourth?" Then he fell back asleep. He died the next day. Incredibly, his old

A view of Jefferson's bedroom at Monticello

friend John Adams died on the same day, hundreds of miles away in Massachusetts. They were the only two signers of the Declaration of Independence to become president.

Virginia

Today, Virginia is home to more than six million people. Its largest city is Virginia Beach, and its capital is Richmond. Monticello, Thomas Jefferson's home near Charlottesville, is open to the public. Charlottesville is also home to the University of Virginia.

Charlottesville

Jefferson wanted his epitaph to focus on gifts he gave *to* the people of the United States. He viewed his presidency as a gift he received *from* the people. As a result, he didn't mention it in the epitaph.

Thomas Jefferson is buried in a family graveyard just down the mountainside from his home. The grave site is maintained by the Monticello Association, which is made up of Jefferson's descendants.

Before he died in 1826, Jefferson wrote detailed instructions for his grave. He sketched a design for his tombstone. He also wrote his own epitaph (memorial statement), which was placed on his grave. It reads: "Here was buried Thomas Jefferson, author of the Declaration of American Independence, of the statute of Virginia for religious freedom, and father of the University of Virginia."

In Your Community

Thomas Jefferson was a master of words and ideas. Jefferson used them to change the world he lived in. Do you have ideas about how to make your community a better place? They don't have to be big ideas, like Jefferson's. Even small changes are important. Jefferson helped start the Library of Congress. Are there ways you can support your local library? Of course, the library

Timeline

1743 — Thomas Jefferson is born on April 2 in Goochland County, Virginia.

1760 — Jefferson enrolls in the College of William and Mary.

1762 — Jefferson begins studying law in Williamsburg.

1769 — Jefferson is elected to the Virginia House of Burgesses.

1772 — Jefferson marries Martha Wayles Skelton on New Year's Day; Martha "Patsy" Jefferson is born.

1774 — Jefferson writes *A Summary View of the Rights of British America*.

1775 — Jefferson is elected to the Second Continental Congress.

1775–1783 — The American Revolutionary War is fought.

1776 — Jefferson writes the Declaration of Independence.

1778 — Mary "Polly" Jefferson is born.

is also a great place to learn about other causes that you can support.

Jefferson also loved to garden. Can you volunteer your time for the local garden society? Perhaps you have a grandparent or neighbor with a garden. He or she might appreciate your company and help with planting, weeding, and watering. Ask a teacher or another adult to help you find creative ways to improve your community.

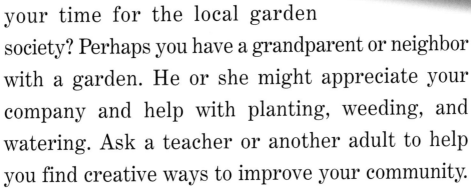

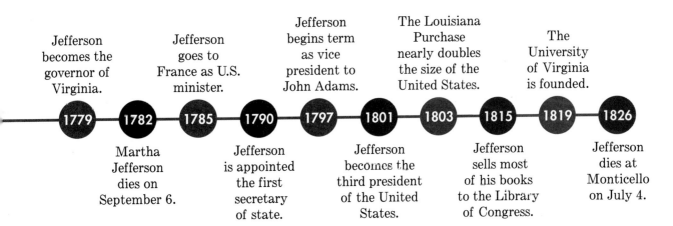

Jefferson becomes the governor of Virginia.

Jefferson goes to France as U.S. minister.

Jefferson begins term as vice president to John Adams.

The Louisiana Purchase nearly doubles the size of the United States.

The University of Virginia is founded.

1779 **1782** **1785** **1790** **1797** **1801** **1803** **1815** **1819** **1826**

Martha Jefferson dies on September 6.

Jefferson is appointed the first secretary of state.

Jefferson becomes the third president of the United States.

Jefferson sells most of his books to the Library of Congress.

Jefferson dies at Monticello on July 4.

To Find Out More

Here are some additional resources to help you learn more about Thomas Jefferson, the American Revolution, Monticello, Virginia, and more:

Books

Kent, Deborah. *Lexington and Concord.* Children's Press, 1997.

Morris, Jeffrey. *The Jefferson Way.* Lerner, 1994.

Nardo, Don. *Thomas Jefferson.* Lucent Books, 1993.

Richards, Norman. *Monticello.* Children's Press, 1995.

Sakurai, Gail. *The Library of Congress.* Children's Press, 1998.

Organizations and Online Sites

Library of Congress
101 Independence Avenue, SE
Washington, DC 20540
http://www.loc.gov
The world's largest library, the Library of Congress contains more than 100 million items in three separate buildings. The library's website includes general information about the library, a database, and interesting special exhibits.

Thomas Jefferson Memorial Foundation
P.O. Box 316
Charlottesville, Virginia 22902
http://www.monticello.org
Visit Jefferson's beloved home online. If you're a student, you can even post a letter to Mr. Jefferson on the "Ask Thomas Jefferson" page.

National Archives and Records Administration
7th Street and Pennsylvania Avenue, NW
Washington, DC 20408
http://www.nara.gov
Visit the site's online Exhibit Hall for the complete text of the Declaration of Independence.

Index

About the Author

Andrew Santella is a lifelong resident of Chicago, Illinois. He is a graduate of Chicago's Loyola University, where he studied American literature. He writes magazine articles about books, sports, and other topics. For Children's Press, he has written several books for series including Community Builders, Cornerstones of Freedom, and Sports Stars.

Since Mr. Santella enjoys reading and writing about architecture, politics, and history, Thomas Jefferson was a fascinating subject. Charlottesville, Virginia, is one of the author's favorite travel destinations.